The Undiscovered Room

The Undiscovered Room

Poems by
Jo McDougall

TAVERN BOOKS

PORTLAND

Cover art: Sean Healy, *American Muscle (sky-blue convertible)*,
2014. Resin-coated cigarette filters. 40" x 40".
Copyright © Sean Healy. Courtesy of Private Collection,
the Artist, and Elizabeth Leach Gallery.

Jo McDougall, 1935-

ISBN-13: 978-1-935635-55-0 (paperback)
ISBN-13: 978-1-935635-56-7 (hardcover)

LCCN: 2015957344

FIRST EDITION

98765432 First Printing

TAVERN BOOKS
Union Station
800 NW 6th Avenue #255
Portland, Oregon 97209
www.tavernbooks.org

Poems

I / Rustling the Blinds

II / Important Bones

III / Sweet Contrivances

IV / Stillness Falling like Calamity

For Charles
and
in memory of Miller Williams,
teacher and friend

love is more thicker than forget
—e e cummings

I

Rustling the Blinds

A Way with Mules

I don't like writing about the dead,
conjuring them in language
that some of them
never would have used—
pushing them onstage,
saying, "Go. It doesn't have to be the truth."
Something's varnished about it,
all klieg lights and rouge,
all glistery shadows.
Yet, what else is there to do?
Shouldn't you, Reader,
be led to see these glossy, passionate,
stumping souls
who once plowed a field in the teeth of a tornado,
waltzed with a wooden leg,
sashayed an armadillo on a leash?

Perhaps not. Perhaps you've already left the page,
dealing with your own ghosts,
throwing them over your shoulder like salt:
a cousin, a brother missing in action
who smoked every day a pack of Camels
and had a way with mules.

Vehicle

Nobody wants to be a ghost.
It's tiresome, being noticed
but never seen.
How else can one go back, though,
to the house that was sold or burned
or rotted away—
to rustle the blinds,
startle the cat,
walk barefoot out
for the morning paper?

In a Muddy Town

She was my classmate in a muddy town,
an uncle they say for a father,
skinny in a bad dress.
No one noticed
a dream or two lost.
No one knew
when she first came to understand,
in those moored rooms
surrounded by fields of vetch,
that a page had turned,
that her life had dimmed
to the colors of snow
or rabbits or celery.

Poverty

Every visit to that farm,
I smelled it:
Sun flailing the flint rocks. The red dirt.
Rusty water in the well. The Garrett snuff
my grandfather dipped,
the too-small suit they buried him in,
the Church of the Newborn, its one
drafty window.
The young preacher late,
borrowed from another county.

Stepping Stones

My young father laid them
about the farmhouse grounds
so my mother could keep above the mud,
crisscrossing from kitchen to clothesline
to chickens to pole beans.

Her steps, mine,
my father's and sister's
polished them down,
but still they marched in place
through time and weeds
until they led nowhere.

Tonight, in a dream,
they take me to the garden, the sheds.
Renewed, they gleam,
as necessary as harvest,
Sundays,
the pistol to the lame horse's head.

Bringing In the Sheaves

It's 1945. The crops laid by
in October if he was lucky,
by Thanksgiving if not,
my father would throw his hat into the threshing machine
with the final shock of rice
from the final field.
That one moment of the year
he was jubilant, cocky even,
winning out
over creditors and blackbirds and rot.
Then the December rains,
the hunger for rattling machinery,
for sweat, for missing crews—
wasted months of accounting and tinkering.
He would have cut off his thumb and buried it,
had he thought that would hasten spring.
Then, spring—
when, laying his plow to the insolent dirt,
he began again.

Green Slopes

The house of my grandparents,
austere as an antler,
why did I love it?
With its needy doors and its yard dirt,
its one magnolia that never blossomed,
its women—my grandmother, my aunt—
coming after supper from their posts in the kitchen
to the front porch,
giving the dark some starch,
their voices destined to drift
across green slopes that never existed,
clear ponds and fields
I'm obliged to invent.

Stairs

My girlfriend's porch had stairs
made of soggy pine,
sorry in a sorry part of town,
leading down into a balding yard
where she and I at eight or nine
bewitched frogs to emeralds, sticks to wands.

I remember those stairs
as solid oak,
leading into a shade of elms,
an organza skim of dragonflies,
no frogs in sight—
and no one cursing,
no one making bruises on us,
demoting our spirits to bile.

I remember that town as regal,
its houses like dowagers—
where we never had jobs at the shoe plant
or men
who smelled of Vienna sausages and diesel.

Memory, So Sleek and Practiced,

commands my senses—
those lazeabouts lolling like summer snakes
beside some stagnant stream—
to listen up. They do,
yawning, preening, thinking themselves
masters of the day.
Then earthquake, tornado, tsunami,
as memory brings me you,
bright and smoldering as a caesar.

Bequest

Sometimes my mother comes to dance with me
around the kitchen table,
wearing the fur coat she bought
when she ran off to Chicago, taking me through steps
I'll never learn.

I wish she had died old and proper,
after she'd taught me waltzes and a few songs.
But she is young always in a silver frame,
her hand to her chin in that elegant way
she never bothered to pass down.

Seeing on the Horizon This Day My Death

This day my town
withers into its shadow,

having no grasses, trees,
no streets named Ellenwood or Teal,

no places like the one
I was accustomed to duck into

from the rising dark,
finding the small fireplace,

the coat rack with its peeling paint,
somebody who knew my name.

II

Important Bones

A Fair Day

Today we lay my mother in her grave,
a fair day,
spring clanking its old cliches:
a willow stammering into leaf,
lawns stupefied with green.

My mother's perfume
crumples the air
and I am five again,
spring an undiscovered room
glimpsed through the scrim of her hair
as she bends to help me tie my Sunday shoes.
A neighbor's basketball
punishes a sidewalk,
a breeze memorizes the curtains
in that world, magical
as waterfalls in Oklahoma.

The soloist sings "Rock of Ages,"
my mother's favorite hymn.
The preacher lays down words
like cutlery on a table.

Her Husband Stricken,
a Bottomlands Farmer's Wife Calls 911

As I put down the phone,
the noise in my head
erases my kitchen:
the counter, the dishes,
the cat food, the cat.

The paramedics take you,
instructing me to follow.
"Which hospital?" they ask. "Lady?"

I direct my charred tongue to speak,
my feet, bound in cement, to find the car
I'd once known how to start.

Not seeing the road, the dark,
I find you
in a hospital named for a saint,
in a room that smells of boiled beets.
I will you to laugh,
throw back the covers.

Under the streetlight,
a steppe of snow.
You don't know my name.

In Due Time

The vet has removed the cat's infected molars
and left him to his bliss.

He will sleep through today and tomorrow.
Then food and naps in his own time,
the front step, then the yard,

where he will find his old self
as the vet has promised,
although no longer able to break
the important bones of birds.

At the Sunny Day Cafe

I order coffee and watch a fly
dance itself close to death
on the windowsill.
I think of my daughter, dying,
her breath a noisy braiding of air.
That was a day in March. The twenty-first day.

The sun dissolves behind a cloud.
The fly, magnificent now, sizzles.

Leaving the Summer Rental
Near Bar Harbor, Maine

We fashion a memorial to our daughter,
dead this spring,
and place it on the mantel—
a photograph of that rocky point she claimed,
a heart-shaped stone,
a card with her name—
knowing that little or none of it
will endure
those who may come here after us:
a novelist
mistaking the stone for a paperweight,
a couple on their honeymoon
disbelieving death,
the cleaning woman tossing it all out
with the milk and cigarettes.

Talking with My Dead Daughter (1)

Today I read of an artist who uses dust
from the homes of her subjects
to paint their portraits,
mixing it with bright oils.

Why did I not think of this?
Dust from your grave
so bright and powdery
it would warble like sunlit mica

as I smeared the canvas with my hands,
tracing your bones and smile and body,
the pandemonium of your hair.

Talking with My Dead Daughter (2)

Why do my words fall apart
whenever I describe you?

I was the one Fate chose
to keep you alive, to make the air
remember.
Now and then—minutes, seconds go by—
I don't think of you.
I've failed at grief.

Flat, Outside Memphis

He's young,
gaunt as a gallows,
a woman beside him,
four kids in the back
and him without a spare.
He pulls away, as much as he can,
from the highway.
Mosquitoes rise from the grass.
The woman shouts something to the children,
slams the car door.
It grows dark,
the headlights of passing cars
disinterested as bankers.

In a Delta Courtroom
They Settle the Estate

Like hyenas catching the scent,
the descendants gather at the carcass:
stocks, bonds, fields, owed rent,
the Midas flesh of their father.

Miles away, his idle farm
remembers cows. The house drowns,
filling itself room by room
with the old voices, flailing sounds

of the lost. In vain the sparrows chit.
Nobody left. Nobody listening.

Responsibility

Taking my dog for a walk,
I find four baby possums dead,
their tails curled in question marks,
their mouths eating maggots.

Soon, the April grass around the bodies,
bedazzled until now
with the lark of being grass,
will understand its office
and take them in.

III

Sweet Contrivances

Ruffles and Flourishes

funereal and graceful and glad
—*Charles Bukowski*

Now and again the world sends
its sweet contrivances—
a ruffle of tulip,
raccoons in the attic,
the naked smell of laundry soap.
Apricots. A book's pages after rain.
A blue beetle
fastening a jacket.

Companion

When Grief came to visit,
she hung her skirts and jackets in my closet.
She claimed the one bath.

When I protested,
she assured me it would be
only for a little while.

Then she fell in love with the house,
re-papered the rooms,
laid green carpet in the den.

She's a good listener
and a fiend at double solitaire.
But it's been seven years.

Once I ordered her outright to leave.
Days later
she came back, weeping.

I'd enjoyed my mornings,
coffee for one,
my Tolstoy and Molière.

I asked her in.

White Moons

Because what I thought was the body
in the mousetrap
turned out to be the cheese,
because the can I put in the refrigerator
was Old Dutch Cleanser, not Parmesan,
because I don't know if I have children
or who that man was yesterday
holding my hand,

they've put me here to sit
with dozens of white moons
that someone tells me
are the faces of friends.
But they won't show me their eyes.

Now the moons go out, one by one,
and I beg to go where they are going—
beseeching the brisk woman
who comes morning and night into my room
cheerful as a cockroach.

Amulets

Just before dark
she glances up to see
Death slouched in a doorway,
chain-smoking like a braggart.

When he leaves,
she thinks of lipstick,
the Krupp diamond,
her mother's perfume.

She fancies these,
audacious as wolverines,
fast by the doorframe of each room.

Housewifery

It isn't simple. It never was.
Running a household with hamsters, a python,
a parakeet, a husband, kids.
And now my husband wants to bring home a pig.
"Clean as a whistle," he vows. "You'll never know
she's around."
I will. She'll make demands. She'll want
marinated peelings,
bone china,
her own room.
And won't she be a fine one to attract flies?
I can see it now:
In those five-minute mornings
I call my own,
as I'm having coffee on the deck,
she'll plunk herself down at my desk,
admiring her pedicure,
rifling through my mail.

At the Shell Station

for Gene Ann Newcomer

The checkout girl
smiles at the bike rider
in line behind me.
"Where's your pickup at?"
She laughs.
"You look like an orphan."
I turn. He's young.
"I do?" he stammers,
taking off his helmet.
Earth Mother has found Lost Boy.

Leaving, I see the sun has come to rest
on the girl: her bracelet,
light as a haiku on her wrist,
a button of her dress.

Bad Farmer

Nobody says it
but everybody knows—
grass high in the turn rows,
fences down,
combines late to the fields.
All the farmers shake their heads:
How does he feed his kids?

He curses the weather, the sad machinery,
politics, his father's last will
that chains him to this dirt
dying under his fingernails.

Every morning he goes for coffee,
gossip,
talk of crops and prices
at the Daylight Donut.
When he leaves,
the men grind out their cigarettes,

declare, just under their breaths,
how the man's got a son
strong as an ox, who's never set foot
on a tractor.

One-Horse Store

for Shirley Rosencrantz

Gray as cypress,
flung beside a dirt road
like seed,
it offered tobacco, beer, overalls,
one door open to the heat.

My girlfriend and I,
fifteen and summer-bored,
walked there every day
for Cokes and Little Debbies.
Moving to Hank Williams lonesome on the radio,
we courted the stares of men
old enough to be our fathers,

then sauntered home
to our mothers' wrath,
hoping to God we smelled of booze and cigarettes.

Alone at Flannery O'Connor's Grave on a Night in April, a Woman Hears a Voice

You there—stand back.
If the wind's right, I probably smell,
even after all these years.
Don't give me that simpering look.
You think I made my single bed
and every day sat down
to those mad voices in my head
so you could come around and gawk?

Go away. And take
that maudlin moonlight with you.
Those whippoorwills, too,
sing-sawing like blind men
on their way to the john.

These coins on my grave—
somebody figures how
I'm running out of money here?
Get them out of my sight.

And one more thing—

I'm not hankering to see you,
but if you do come back,
bring a sign for the foot of my grave:
"Spitting Permitted."
Make sure you get the spelling right.

Her Husband Away on a Business Trip, She Takes the Old Pontiac In for Repairs

The young service manager
comes round to explain,
as if someone were dying,

what will have to be done. "It's more,"
he says, "than we thought."
I want to tell him it's all right,

I've heard worse;
we're all orphans here.
Live long enough,

you might as well be a spider
in a corner of the basement,
year in, year out,

marvelously disguised.
But I like this young man
trying to help me understand

that the car is on its last breath.
"Another hour or so, Ma'am,"
he says. "I'm sorry for the wait."

It's all right; I'll be home soon,
perhaps to find you unpacking,
the cat murmuring to himself

like a contented chicken, the radio
waffling through its noise, the replenished Pontiac
exhaling slowly in the drive.

At the Working-Class Hero, Lucinda Williams Gets Her Start

The cafe's screen door slammed
after each customer and every dog
in Fayetteville, Arkansas. Her props:
cigarette smoke and a beat-up guitar.
Seventeen—eighteen, maybe—she wandered among us,
her voice fetching and uneasy,
singing for dollars and nickels
as I passed the hat.
In that camouflage of grease and smoke,
we waited for our futures—
safe, we thought,
the screen door between us
and the trolling dark.

Choice

You've come to the oncologist's office
to talk about your options.
You view the scans,

forgetting to breathe.
"It's metastasized." He frowns,
pointing to where and where.

He ticks off the preferred treatment,
the side effects,
low rates of success.

"It's your choice," he says,
closing your folder,
"but we need to start tomorrow."

You think of yesterday
when you lived in a different universe,
of a waitress,
hand on her hip, asking,

"Hon, you want mustard or mayo
on that sandwich?"

Messenger

A crow I once met
in Peterborough, New Hampshire,
has found me in Kansas City, Missouri—
after navigating the Ohio, the Allegheny, the Monongahela,
the Mississippi
until he came upon (what else) the Kaw.
There he must have stopped for directions
to the intersection of Somerset and State Line,
where he watches as I enter Latte Land—
alerting all comers
that I am here,
then bending to preen,
each feather sending up a hallelujah.

Ceremony

When his wife left, he married the cat.
The courtship was solemn,
carried on by the cat. She'd been
on the fringes—forgotten, discovered,
forgotten again—
and now the rooms were silent
and the man would not speak
but sat flat-footed in his chair.
Then, he accepted her tentative paw
across his shoe.
Then, she climbed onto his lap,
crept under the evening paper.

They came to a blending of ways.
She'd parade to the empty milk dish;
he'd open the carton slowly
for her delight.
Slowly he enjoyed coming home.
His triple knock on the door each evening
became her reason to nip his leg.

Season swung into season.
One night
he lifted her onto the bed, beside him.

She adored the electric blanket,
warm odor of the lampshade.
They fell asleep as the moon rose
to enter a cloud.

A Bottomlands Farmer Takes a Break from Walking His Levees

Rice will grow tall in these fields
if he judges right with his shovel,
opening the levees, closing them,
adjusting the depth of the water.
He's walked these fields all morning,
dodging cottonmouths,
lifting mud and packing it
till it shines like the back of a whale.

At noon, in Brenda's Truck Stop for cigarettes,
he pauses before a case of glass miniatures,
each impossibly small.
The high-noon sun swaggers into Brenda's,
tattooing everything: Excedrin, customers, cotton balls,
t-shirts, the Coke machine, gum.
The window air conditioner shifts down
like an 18-wheeler.
He opens the case,
lifts out an ice-blue, cantering horse.
It stirs in his hands,
light as an eighth note
in a prayer.

Sky of Heartbreak Blue

The towns of Kansas lie under it—
sun scrubbing them to gravel gray,
their stringy lights at night
like stragglers on the prairie,
their citizens grim as barbed wire
and bedazzling.
Entering one of those towns, beware:
The wind will pin you on its main, wide street,
asking questions you don't want to answer.
A church-going town, plain,
its diner full of loneliness
tasting the way cheap whiskey smells.
On closer look, you might like to settle down—
send for the dog and children—
in such a town, so sweet and seething.

IV

Stillness Falling like Calamity

On the Outskirts of Town

Walking in late afternoon,
I saw a fox
trotting toward a stand of trees,
his coat in the slant light
flaming like a young girl's hair.
Seeing me, he froze,
his world banished by my step.

I wished in that moment not to be human,
caught on my course beside the fox's field.
Then he might have nodded to me;
I might have joined him
as the trees formed a ring.

Kansas

Death here has no place to hide:
gunned-down coyotes
stacked in the back of a pickup,
a rabbit flayed and left in the sun.

The folk of Kansas
turn their faces into the snow and rain,
expecting nothing,
slipping their lives into graves
alongside the bulbs of tulips.

Living in Kansas,
I am exiled into light.
Its silence
marries my tongue.

Dinner for Two at an Outdoor Cafe

This is one of those moments
one or the other may remember
when one or the other is gone.
It's June, the trees
as young as they will ever be.

A blue sky narrows to rust.
They linger over coffee,
reluctant to go home
to the predictable chairs and tables,
the family photographs.

Remembering the Brownstone

I want the ring of its iron steps,
ten or eight of them, under my feet—
the banister not quite secure,
the city stuttering around me
like a homeless wind.

I want to hurry up those steps again,
through the double oak dark doors
tall and heavy as God,
want to enter the rooms greeting me like strangers:
aloof, always on the verge of leaving,
shrugging into their polite coats.

Cemetery at Flat Bayou

Loud as butchering,
rain and frogs settle
beside my daughter.
In the trees above her grave
the hoot owls turn the air to oil,
so many of them, so many calls.

Seeking Absolution, a Woman Addresses the Past Once Again

Like the pastor
who never blesses his flock
Or the wife who withdraws
till all desire is gone to grief

Or grief, which,
like an enormous portrait
over the mantel,
stares every living thing
to stone,
you remain unmoved.

Must I pave the Sahara?
Weave water?
Stitch through snow?

These I have done,
and still you roam the halls
like a fog of cholera.

Old Loves

We forgive them
but they intrude
in the way that a woman
smashes the six settings
of her mother's antique Spode
at a garden party, alongside the verbena.

Ingrates

I'm standing at an airport gate,
staring back at the staring windows.
A sparrow, lost,
berates itself for its mistake,
lurching again and again at the ceiling.

A voice falls out of the intercom,
speaking in gravel,
and we queue up to board—sullen,
as if begrudging this transport from earth,
interrupted in our important lives.

The sparrow tries again,
its wings thickening.

Notes on the Death of a Child

Insult.
Bone bruise.
Death's stinger left
in the roof of my mouth.

Smallsong

O what is the weather today, the day
I go to bury my daughter

And what shall I wear today, the day
I'll stand at the grave of my daughter

O who is that beggar in my way
As I walk to the church for my daughter

And why does he sing
O who will give me a dollar

As the bells ring
For my daughter

A Man Considers the Ways of Love

He removes a toy
from the wood floor
so the floor will not have to endure it.

Removes a rug
lest an old woman topple.

Extracts the fish bone
before the unsuspecting diner lifts his fork.

Turns away from music
so silence might have him in thrall.

Thinks of cows,
well fed, well grazed,
the care we give
those we have sentenced to fall.

A Woman Considers Relativity

When she thinks of her grandmother,
who'd never before come near the furnace,
approaching in terror to light it
the winter her husband died—

or a friend capsizing with cancer,
or herself, sidling up to death,
its scaly rancor,

then betrayals,
words like cat-o'-nine-tails,
ties riven in anger
pale—elbowed aside, upstaged.

New House

The whir of a dove's wing evaporates,
and I am left on a floe of silence
as if I were deaf or mute
or had lost verbs
and any tongue to taste them,
as if I had moved from place to place
too often, and wrong.

Woman Ironing

As I walk down a street
as quiet as a crypt,
a moment solidifies into stone.
A rabbit, halting midway across a lawn,
turns to me
one onyx-perfect eye.
A woman ironing,
framed by an open window,
sighs and shifts her weight,
alone with her thoughts.
She cannot know she is consigned
to this August day
to drift in and out
the long faults of my memory.

Watching *Casablanca*
in Arkadelphia, Arkansas

It's 3 a.m.
Fog permeates Casablanca
as fog floats above the Ouachita,
the river this town lies ragtag along.
Those flimmering creatures on the screen are dead,
the town at this hour is dead,
the vapor of that river rises
to touch my feet.
Now the early morning train
clangoring through Arkadelphia.
I stumble toward my coat and my valise.
I must be gone
before the Germans,
the closed borders,
the informant sun.
O Ingrid, Humphrey, Sydney, Paul,
shadows on the banks of my life,
I point the remote and exile you all.

The Studio

I had heard of Hemingway's time in Piggott, Arkansas—
a studio in a barn, a famous manuscript.
Now, invited to these grounds,
I enter the studio.
November niggles the grass, the trees
as Hemingway stands at his typewriter, his back to me,
papers scattered like lilies across a pond.
As he walks toward a wall
where the heads of animals have come to die again,
one, an impala, finds the rest of its body and slips it on,
kicking the studio into a maelstrom of dust
that moves like a gasp to slather Piggott,
erasing the town square
and the last evening train.

The next morning, I ask around.
No one has noticed an impala on the loose
or extra dust. Folks ply the square idly and complain
of the train last night splitting their sleep as usual,
the lunch special at Donna's, the threat of rain.

I make my way to the studio. The windows are there,
the door, the roof.
An old lion in a stutter of sun, it sits
glinting and implacable.

Lawn

Unable to sleep,
she walks onto the lawn,
cold and ivory under the moon.
An owl makes its stiff noise.
Something whispers across her feet.
Stepping inside,
she's caught in the lawn's slow spell,
as if a swimmer, drowned,
had been pulled to shore—
a crowd gathering,
stillness falling like calamity.

Ambition, Late Life

No Alps are here, no gold.
No Byzantium, no silver streets.
Only a few deer
lifting their heads,
then bowing to the grass.

Scolds

In rooms the color of winter
you encounter your dreams:
the ones that toggle inside you,
the ones that haven't yet found you,
the ones sleeping in closets of houses
you've long forgot.
Against these walls,
they fidget like the wings of a wasp.
And there in a doorway the one dream,
tapping her foot.

Acknowledgments

Grateful acknowledgment is made to the editors of the following publications in which these poems, some in different versions, first appeared:

Arkansas Review: "Choice"; "The Studio"; "On the Outskirts of Town"

Arts & Letters: "A Bottomlands Farmer Takes a Break from Walking His Levees"; "In a Delta Courtroom They Settle the Estate"

The Broadkill Review, online: "Bad Farmer"; "Cemetery at Flat Bayou"; "Dinner for Two at an Outdoor Cafe"; "At the Shell Station"; "Poverty"

The Broomweed Journal: "Woman Ironing," also reprinted in *The Midwest Quarterly*

Coal Hill Review, online: "Remembering the Brownstone"

Columbia Poetry Review: "Talking with My Dead Daughter (1)"; "Talking with My Dead Daughter (2)"; "Responsibility"

Court Green: "One-Horse Store"

Flint Hills Review: "Bringing In the Sheaves"; "Her Husband Stricken, a Bottomlands Farmer's Wife Calls 911"

The Fourth River: "A Fair Day"; "Leaving the Summer Rental Near Bar Harbor, Maine"

Ghoti, online: "At the Sunny Day Cafe"; "Green Slopes" (as "House"); "Watching *Casablanca* in Arkadelphia, Arkansas"

I-70 Review: "In a Muddy Town"; "Stepping Stones"; "Stairs"; "Ruffles and Flourishes"; "Seeking Absolution, a Woman Addresses the Past Once Again"; "Ambition, Late Life"

Kansas City Star: "Vehicle" (as "Going Back")

Margie: "Flat, Outside Memphis"; "Notes on the Death of a Child"

The Midwest Quarterly: "Lawn"; "White Moons"; "Sky of Heartbreak Blue," also reprinted in *Scythe*, online; "Memory, So Sleek and Practiced,"; "At the Working-Class Hero, Lucinda Williams Gets Her Start"; "A Man Considers the Ways of Love"; "A Woman Considers Relativity"; "Ingrates"; "Housewifery"; "Messenger"; "Smallsong"; "New House"; "Woman Ironing" (reprinted from *The Broomweed Journal*)

MiPOesias, online: "A Way with Mules" (as "Summoning the Lost"), also reprinted in *Daddy's Money: A Memoir of Farm and Family* (University of Arkansas Press)

New Century North American Poets, ed. John Garmon, Donna Biffar, and Wayne Lanter (River King Press): "In Due Time"

New Letters: "Bequest" (as "A Woman Remembers Her Mother, Who Died Young"); "Alone at Flannery O'Connor's Grave on a Night in April, a Woman Hears a Voice"

Nimrod: "Old Loves" (as "Poems")

Parachute, online: "Amulets" (as "Charms")

Scythe, online: "Seeing on the Horizon This Day My Death"; "Kansas"; "Sky of Heartbreak Blue" (reprinted from *The Midwest Quarterly*)

The Sixth Surface: Steven Holl Lights the Nelson-Atkins Museum, ed. J.M. Rees (topo/graphis press): "Scolds" (as "Lanterns")

Today's Alternative News, online: "Ceremony"

2River View, online: "Companion," also reprinted in *She Walks in Beauty: A Woman's Journey Through Poems*, ed. Caroline Kennedy (Hyperion/Harper Collins); "Her Husband Away on a Business Trip, She Takes the Old Pontiac In for Repairs"

I'm grateful to Carl Adamshick and Natalie Garyet at Tavern Books for their belief in, and close editing of, my work; to Stephen Meats, Michael Simms, William Trowbridge, and the late Miller Williams for invaluable suggestions during the development of this manuscript; to Greg Field, Lola Haskins, Sam Hazo, M Ross Henry, Collin McDougall, Merritt McDougall, Eva Simms, Alarie Tennille, Maryfrances Wagner, and Jordan Williams for thoughtful input on many of these poems; to Alice Friman, Andrea Hollander, Maryalice Hurst, Tom Lavoie, M. J. Melneck, and Elwood (Turk) Smith for ongoing support; to Chris Purcell, Polly Rosenwaike and Carol Sickman-Garner for word-by-word reading; to Beth Brubaker for generous technical support.

As always, special gratitude goes to my husband, Charles, for his enduring patience, counsel, and honest criticism.

Tavern Books

Tavern Books is a not-for-profit poetry publisher that exists to print, promote, and preserve works of literary vision, to foster a climate of cultural preservation, and to disseminate books in a way that benefits the reading public.

We publish books in translation from the world's finest poets, champion new works by innovative writers, and revive out-of-print classics. We keep our titles in print, honoring the cultural contract between publisher and author, as well as between publisher and public. Our catalog, known as The Living Library, sustains the visions of our authors, ensuring their voices remain alive in the social and artistic discourse of our modern era.

The Living Library

Arthur's Talk with the Eagle by Anonymous,
translated from the Welsh by Gwyneth Lewis

Ashulia by Zubair Ahmed

Breckinridge County Suite by Joe Bolton

*My People & Other Poems by Wojciech Bonowicz,
translated from the Polish by Piotr Florczyk

Buson: Haiku by Yosa Buson,
translated from the Japanese by Franz Wright

Evidence of What Is Said by Ann Charters and Charles Olson

Who Whispered Near Me by Killarney Clary

The End of Space by Albert Goldbarth

Six-Minute Poems: The Last Poems
by George Hitchcock

The Wounded Alphabet: Collected Poems
by George Hitchcock

Hitchcock on Trial
by George Hitchcock

*The Boy Changed into a Stag Clamors
at the Gate of Secrets* by Ferenc Juhász,
translated from the Hungarian by David Wevill

My Blue Piano by Else Lasker-Schüler,
translated from the German by Eavan Boland

Why We Live in the Dark Ages by Megan Levad

Prodigy by Charles Simic,
drawings by Charles Seluzicki

Night of Shooting Stars by Leonardo Sinisgalli,
translated from the Italian by W. S. Di Piero

Skin by Tone Škrjanec,
translated from the Slovene by Matthew Rohrer and Ana Pepelnik

We Women by Edith Södergran,
translated from the Swedish by Samuel Charters

Winterward by William Stafford

Building the Barricade by Anna Świrszczyńska,
translated from the Polish by Piotr Florczyk

Baltics by Tomas Tranströmer
with photographs by Ann Charters,
translated from the Swedish by Samuel Charters

For the Living and the Dead by Tomas Tranströmer,
translated from the Swedish by John F. Deane

Prison by Tomas Tranströmer
with a postscript by Jonas Ellerström,
translated from the Swedish by Malena Mörling

Tomas Tranströmer's First Poems &
Notes From the Land of Lap Fever
by Tomas Tranströmer
with a commentary by Jonas Ellerström,
translated from the Swedish by Malena Mörling

Casual Ties by David Wevill

Where the Arrow Falls by David Wevill

Collected Translations by David Wevill

Night is Simply a Shadow by Greta Wrolstad

Notes on Sea & Shore by Greta Wrolstad

The Countries We Live In by Natan Zach,
translated from the Hebrew by Peter Everwine

*forthcoming

Tavern Books is funded, in part, by the generosity of philanthropic organizations, public and private institutions, and individual donors. By supporting Tavern Books and its mission, you enable us to publish the most exciting poets from around the world. To learn more about underwriting Tavern Books titles, please contact us by e-mail: info@tavernbooks.org.

MAJOR FUNDING HAS BEEN PROVIDED BY

THE PUBLICATION OF THIS BOOK IS MADE POSSIBLE, IN PART, BY THE SUPPORT OF THE FOLLOWING INDIVIDUALS

Gabriel Boehmer

Dean & Karen Garyet

Mark Swartz & Jennifer Jones

The Mancini Family

Mary Ann Ryan

Marjorie Simon

Bill & Leah Stenson

Dan Wieden

Ron & Kathy Wrolstad

Colophon

This book was designed and typeset by Eldon Potter at Bryan Potter Design, Portland, Oregon. The text is set in Garamond, an old-style serif typeface named for the punch-cutter Claude Garamond (c. 1480-1561). Display font is Manifold, designed by Connary Fagen. *The Undiscovered Room* appears in both paperback and cloth-covered editions. Printed on archival-quality paper by McNaughton & Gunn, Inc.